GUI GU ZI

WISDOM
OF THE
Ghost Valley

COMPOSED BY WANG XU;
TRANSLATED BY JACK SUN

outskirts
press

Wisdom of the Ghost Valley
Gui Gu Zi
All Rights Reserved.
Copyright © 2020 Composed by Wang Xu; Translated by Jack Sun
v1.0

Outskirts Press, Inc.
http://www.outskirtspress.com

ISBN: 978-1-9772-2161-2

PRINTED IN THE UNITED STATES OF AMERICA

For all who aspire to succeed in an ethical and legal way

TABLE OF CONTENTS

Introduction

Gui Gu Zi, or Wisdom of the Ghost Valley in modern English, is a compilation of Daoism philosophy and Persuasion Techniques, which were written about 2,400 years ago. Though the exact author is still a topic of debate among scholars, several trustworthy evidences points to the fact that a hidden sage, whose name was Wang Xu, lived in the ghost valley (modern He Nan in China) and composed this book that incorporated Daoism, School of Naturalists, and School of Diplomacy. Perhaps due to his belief on secrecy and mysteriousness, he meditated in solitude. However, it is said that he lived for more than one hundred years and was the mentor to some of the most distinguished political and military figures in the Warring States Period in ancient China. Su Qin, Zhang Yi, Sun Bin, and Pang Juan, to name a few. A few chapters of Gui Gu Zi is now lost due to ages, but numerous Chinese intellectuals in the past have read and annotated it. For some, it was a priceless treatise on military and diplomatic strategies that can dominate the world if used appropriately. But for others, it was nothing more than a flattering scum's pocketbook on manipulation and deception. It is necessary for you, the modern reader, to carefully read, think, and reflect on the genuine messages behind each word in the book, and employ the core teachings of the author to real world circumstances in an ethically acceptable way. I, as a translator, do not guarantee definite results because it varies based on your mindset, belief, attitude, philosophy and experience. If you truly WANT to succeed in your life and understand the POWER of words, then this book, Gui Gu Zi, is an invaluable asset for you. Read on. And I wish you the best of luck.

A Portrait of Wang Xu

Chapter 1.

Bai He

(Openness and Closedness)

Examining the history of the past, the Great Man, who lives amongst the heaven and earth, is the lord of all beings. By observing the changes of the aspects of Yin and Yang, he makes predictions and judgments about them, understands the ways of life and death, plans everything from the beginning to the end, knows the doctrine of human psychology, and predicts the signs of changes in order to understand its core concepts. So the purpose of the Great Man has always been the same throughout history. Although all beings have no definite limitation of changes, they all have their final destinations. They can be either yin or yang; weak or strong; openness or closedness; softness or intensity.

Therefore, the Great Man should always understand, observe and apply the core principle of changes of all beings in order to measure the intelligence and ability of his opponents. As for people's kindness, incompetence, wisdom, stupidity, courage, cowardliness, and justice, they all differentiate from one another. So, he can either open or close, advance or retreat, respect or despite, depend on the principle of "Wu Wei" (compliance with natural principles instead of artificial interference) to control his opponents. For instance, he shall test their truthfulness and deceitfulness, and know their hobbies and desires in order to accurately predict their ambitions and motivations. In addition, he can also mildly disagree with the arguments of his opponents, and then wait to rebuke after they have revealed themselves in order to know the factual intelligence. The most valuable part is understanding their true intentions behind their words and behaviors, and then remain silent to provoke them to speak in order to capture their core weaknesses. The Great Man, then, can either show off his ambition, philosophy, mindsets, emotions, characters, habits, behaviors, or simply remain silent to hide them. The purpose to show off his personalities is because his matches his opponents', and the purpose to remain silent is because his differs from his opponents'. To decide whether the outcome is beneficial, the Great Man must understand his opponents' strategies in order to assess the similarities and differences between him and them. These strategies and motivations can vary, but he must remain adamant about his own thoughts and ideas. If the situation is favorable, he should comply his opponents' will first.

If he wants to utilize the way of "Bai" (openness), it is crucial to be thoroughly prepared. If he wants to utilize the way of "He" (closedness), it is crucial to maintain utmost secrecy. Therefore, the importance of preparation and secrecy almost parallels to that of the "Dao" (The Great Way). To make his opponents open their mouths is to evaluate their true intentions. To make his opponents close their mouths is to affirm their honesty and motives. The purpose of all of these moves is to reveal their abilities and strategies in order to better assess his potential gains and losses. Such is how the Great Man thinks. If he cannot determine his opponents' capabilities or data, he will be distressed. As a result of "openness", he can either show off himself or accept his opponents' reactions. As for that of "closedness", he can either obtain his opponents' intelligence or abandon this situation. "Openness" and "closedness" are the principles of heaven and earth. "Openness" and "closedness" are also the guiding forces of the changes of yin and yang and the beginning and end of the four seasons to stimulate the evolution of all beings. No matter any changes, repetitions, or paradoxes, they follow the law of "Bai" and "He".

"Openness" and "Closedness" are not only the law of the universe, but also the foundation of the Persuasion Techniques. It is crucial to scrutinize and observe their changes beforehand. The tongue is the doorway to the mind, and the mind is the core of the soul. Motivation, ambition, preference, desire, thought, concern, intelligence and strategy all come from this source. Therefore, it is necessary to use the way of "Bai" and "He" to guard this doorway in order to control the ebbs and flows of words.

The categories of "Bai" consists of openness, talk, and yang. The categories of "He" consists of closedness, silence, and yin. Harmonious synergy of yin and yang result in the balance of "openness" and "closedness". Therefore, long life, peace, happiness, richness, prosperity, respect, honor, significance, reputation, love, preference, wealth, benefit, gain, wish, hobby, and desire attribute to "yang" and are named "beginning". Correspondingly, death, anxiety, uneasiness, poverty, despicableness, suffering, humiliation, abandonment, destruction, depression, bankruptcy, hopelessness, disaster, persecution, massacre, and punishment attribute to "yin" and are named "end". Those who follow and employ the persuasive languages of "yang" are called the beginners that speak the words of "benevolence" to commence objectives. Those who follow and employ the persuasive languages of "yin" are called the enders that speak the words of "malevolence" to terminate strategies.

The way of "Bai" and "He" can be experimented from both aspects of yin and yang. As a result, treat "beginners" with handsome rewards and honorable respect. Treat "enders" with inferior rewards and shameful disrespect. Use the lowly techniques to appeal the enders and use lofty techniques to appeal the beginners. Nothing cannot be understood, examined, or accomplished by using this Persuasion Technique. It can also be used to persuade and influence people, family, country and the whole world. There is no limitation of "internal aspects" in regard of small accomplishments. There is no limitation of "external aspects" in regard of big accomplishments. All losses, gains, departures, arrivals, betrayals, and returns can be manipulated by the law of yin and yang. Yang moves and you advance, whereas yin stops and you withdraw. Yang moves and you invade, whereas yin conceals and you infiltrate. All yang eventually end in yin and all yin eventually alter to yang. Those who live with yang will enhance their

   WISDOM OF THE GHOST VALLEY

characters. Those who live with yin will form behavioral patterns. To appeal yin with yang, you must accept them with virtue and generosity. To attract yang with yin, you must demonstrate your external power and appeal. The reason why yin and yang attract and connect is because of the law of "Bai" and "He". Such is the principle of the universe and the methodology of the Persuasion Technique. It is also the origin of all matters and subjects, which is why it is called the "Doorway to the Heaven and Earth".

Chapter 2.

反應

(Contradictory Response)

The Great Man of ancient times who preached the way of "Dao" and nurtured all beings, flourished harmoniously with the evolution of the nature. He reviewed and observed the way of "Dao" to examine the patterns of history and forecast the trends of future; he remembered and understood the way of "Dao" to learn the lessons of the past and foresee the tendency of the future; he also comprehended and applied the way of "Dao" to discern the intentions and strategies of his opponents and reflect upon himself. If the principle of movement, stillness, emptiness and fullness are all inapplicable in the present time, you should learn from the past experiences and antecedent pioneers. Some knowledge, principles, and wisdom can only be obtained after repetitive examinations, mistakes and experiences. The Great Man assessed such conclusion, which must be carefully studied and contemplated.

When people speak, they are in the status of movement. When you are silent, you are in the status of stillness. Therefore, you should perceive the true meaning behind their words. If their languages are conflicting or inappropriate to your benefits or mentality, you can castigate and denounce them, who will then certainly argue back. Languages can be imitated, whereas objects can be correlated. These two can then be used to predict people's speeches and behaviors. The theory is to imitate objects and compare arguments. The practice is to discern opponents' audible languages with soundless and formless principles. Utilize teasing words and behaviors to provoke their truthful responses in order to fathom their facts. Such tactic is similar to capture a wild beast with a net: the hunter should prepare and ambush his prey with plentiful nets and wait till it falls to the trap. Applying the same beast-trapping technique to any relationships, the opponents will naturally reveal themselves. This is called the "Human-Netting-Strategy". If they still show no signs of difference in words, verbal or body languages that can be used to compare with your anticipation, then it is best to change your own strategy. As an illustration, you shall use any objects of interest to appeal them in order to determine their thoughts and emotions, which then can be exploited to reveal their facts and intentions that will further be manipulated to completely dominate them. You shall also remain silent and often change your prospective to cause your opponents to react and comply. And then it will be easier to speculate their next moves and responses, thus fortifying your confidence. Continually pressing verbal assaults on the opponents for countless repetitions to discern and know every facts and intelligences about them from their mere words. The Great Man, therefore, can tempt either the wise or the fool and he will always receive all factual information from them and remain doubtless.

The ancient masters, who could listen and speculate from a critical perspective and an astute mindset, could learn all the information and intelligences from the faintest traces and the most mysterious sources. The opponents can change, adjust and adapt like the shapeless water, so it is imperative to match and control them with your meticulous assessments. If no research or understanding is prepared, then the resulting intelligence will be uncertain and jeopardizing. Such is the cause of doubtful mentality and weak foundation. Changing objects of interest and languages of comparison will definitely yield contrary arguments from the opponents, who must be carefully listened and observed. For example, you can remain silent to provoke them to speak; you can withdraw yourself to encourage them to advance; you can descend your position before reaching the summit; and you can present reciprocity while anticipating returns. In order to reveal the opponents' true strategies, it is imperative to use the techniques of "imitation" and "correlation" to comprehend and further control their minds behind their languages. And then, voices and tones of identical nature will emerge as a result of mutual communication and understanding, which guarantee truthful insights and information. Applying the principle of such techniques, you can serve your superior while managing your subordinates. This is the way of differentiating between the real and the fake, friend and foe, true enemy intel and treacherous deceptions. All actions, behaviors, languages, and silence will be revealed through imitation and correlation. All emotions such as joy, anger and fear can be discerned from the same source. Judgment is made through predetermination and forecast, backed with data and intel. You should utilize the reverse perspective to appeal for your opponents' responses while observing their psychological weight and priority. You should also achieve inner peace first to listen to your opponents' languages, examine their activities, discuss about fauna and flora, and distinguish between male and female. Although the discussion is not about the main topic, you can easily perceive the broad picture of totality from just the very details of the surface. This concept is similar to spying on enemies' intelligence and camouflaging within the enemies' territory: estimate their might and abilities first and then understand their motivation. Its efficiency parallels to the reliability of the ancient Aquila, velocity of a winged serpent, and accuracy of the mighty Achilles.

Therefore, the first step to know someone is to know thyself. After possessing self-knowledge, the other people can then be comprehended. For instance, communicating and knowing people mirrors the behaviors of flounders. Unveiling their appearance and dancing with your own bear resemblance to the relationship between the light and the shadow. Scrutinizing their languages without inattention or negligence corresponds to using magnet to attract iron needle and chewing meat from a cooked bone, effortless and doubtless. Hardly exposing almost none of your own information while swiftly discerning almost all of your opponents'. It parallels to the fluidity of yin transforming to yang, yang altering to yin, circle changing to square and square reversing back to circle. When the opponents have not revealed themselves or the situations are unclear, it is necessary to use the strategy of circle, which consists of flexibility and resourcefulness, to shepherd them. When they have revealed themselves or the situations are clear, use the strategy of square, which consists of decisiveness and bravado, to conquer them. No matter they advance, retreat, scheme or scam, you should employ these strategies to adapt and triumph. If you cannot make this decision in advance, then you cannot manage your people well. If you lack the understanding of such techniques that inevitably lead to detrimental incidents, then you are but a leader who "Forsake Virtue and Lose The True Path". On the other head, you should first understand the art of war and relationships, and then apply such skills to manage your people. Utilizing strategies without the faintest traces or the slightest clue---such intelligence is the very definition of War Goddess "Athena".

Chapter 3.

Nei Jian

(Psychological Domination)

THIS IS THE relationship between the superior and the subordinate: some are far away in physical vicinity but close in motivation, mentality and emotions, others are the visa versa. Some subordinates are neglected and distrusted because they constantly approach their superiors with too much aggression and frequency. Others, on the other hand, have been promoted and advanced just because they are gone and absent. Some are not popular or trusted even though they greet their superiors every single day. Others, although separate from great distances, are wanted and remembered simply because their superiors hear their voices. Such relationships can be forged because both of them possess strong inner connections. Therefore, it is crucial to deeply acquainted with your superiors before others do. Methods of establishing such networks include but not limited to: connecting via moral dogma; connecting via friendship or parties; connecting via wealth or compensation; connecting via art or entertainments. If you are the subordinate who want to preach your own philosophy and proposals, you should achieve this level of brilliance: your proposition can quickly invade your superiors' mind and then easily withdraw from it; you can attach or detach with them at will; you can approach or distance them at will; you can even be promoted or remembered by them at will. This concept is similar to the maternal instinct of the wolf spider that raises its offspring: they crawl and scurry with perfect synergy either when they are together or alone. Nothing will stop them.

"Nei" implies using persuasion techniques to influence the superiors, while "Jian" means assuring them to firmly believe and even execute the desired plans and actions. Therefore, the speaker must first carefully measure the strengths and weaknesses of both sides, and the strategist must first deliberately adhere to the superiors' desires and mentalities. Analyzing the feasibility and unfeasibility of each objectives in the shadow, and asserting the gains and losses of each plans in the light in order to completely dominate the superior's ambition and psychology. When they are asking for opinions and strategies, you should response by using such techniques in the right time to comply with theirs. This practice is best applied after every single possibility is considered and before a single word is spoken. Then adjusting it according to the current time, place and circumstance. If your philosophy or strategy mismatch your superiors', you should not commence your plan. Instead, you should meticulously calculate and evaluate the

　　　　WISDOM OF THE GHOST VALLEY

best time and place to speak, then starting from your agreements or their weaknesses to patiently look for an opening to persuade and influence them to your own liking. Those who are excel in manipulating the superiors to make them accept any changes or advices, are the very picture of using the correct key to open door handles, straightforward and uncomplicated. Utilizing the relevant tense and accurate nouns when you are discussing events or people of the past. Similarly, utilizing the appropriate languages and bold claims when you are predicting incidents or changes in the future. For those who want to speak with water-like flexibility, thoroughly understand the geography of target origins first, and then it is plausible to comprehend the way of Heaven, nourish four seasons, vanquish ghosts and gods, harmonize yin and yang, and govern all people.

Only by revealing the true intention and knowing the psychology of the superiors, can you plan your scheme and persuade them with true confidence. On the other hand, any occasions which are not appropriate to the ambition or desire of the superiors is because you only understand the surface level of their plans or personalities, but fail to comprehend their massive "underwater parts of the iceberg". No Great Men will ever plot or speak under such circumstances.

Therefore, those who are distant from their superiors but are acquainted with them, are secretly matching their thoughts in accord. On the contrary, those who are apace with their superiors but are constantly ignored by them, are clearly having different perspectives and objectives than them. Likewise, those who are currently employed by their superiors but have not been handsomely promoted is because their strategies have not accomplished the desired results. Those who have withdrawn from their positions but are rehired by their superiors is because their strategies have proven to be effective and beneficial. Correspondingly, those who greet their superiors every single day but are not deeply trusted is because their manner and demeanor are inappropriate. Those who reside and operate across great distance from their superiors but can be instantaneously remembered just with mere voice, is because their strategies cooperate well with their superiors', who are waiting for them to make vital decisions.

Therefore, those who attempt to lobby before circumstance is crystal clear, are doomed to see their plans fall into oblivion. In the same way, those who attempt to lobby before they understand the core intel, will unquestionably be challenged and ridiculed. As long as you can understand the intelligence about your targets, you will master the art of "Nei Jian". Hence implementing such techniques in your speaking style and then preaching your opinions, you can achieve this degree of excellence: your speech can freely flow in and out from your tongue at your own pleasure; you can either persuade your superiors with iron-hard resolve, or temporarily surrender yourself to adapt to unpredictable environments. As a result, the Great Man, who aspires to accomplish greatness, first masters the art of "Nei Jian" to know the factual information about their opponents, and then dominate all things and all beings.

You shall first approach with their virtue, morality, justice, honesty, courtesy, craving, loyalty, trustworthiness, thoughtfulness and strategy. And then cite from the Classic of Poetry and the Book

　　　WISDOM OF THE GHOST VALLEY

of Documents about teachings and wisdom. Furthermore, you shall also evaluate the advantages and disadvantages of each possibilities before making the final decision of acceptance or denial for your employment. If you want to collaborate with people, utilize their needs, wants, and greed to your favor. If you want to withdraw from your current position, utilize the impacts of events, affairs, and conflicts as your edges. When dealing with people of outstanding triumph or events of great magnitude, it is necessary to understand the principles and methods about persuasion and negotiation. When forecasting incidents or changes in the future, it is crucial to make quick and decisive judgments in uncertain situations. Perfectly executing flawless strategies, continually achieving glory and significance, and ceaselessly accumulating righteousness and rectitude. All of these steps are used for managing civilians well in order to stimulate them to boost greater manufactory and productivity. Such is the interpretation of a harmonized relationship between subordinates and their superiors. On the contrary, If either the superiors are too corrupted or incompetent to administer decisions, or the subordinates are so chaotic and anarchic that impair their duties, the undeniable results would be: subordinates affirm their own opinions and incentives while severely clashing with each other on every single subject; they together perceive themselves to be the pinnacle of absolute greatness while neglecting new ideas or technologies. Their arrogant, over-praising behaviors on themselves create a turbulent environment. Under this circumstance, if you are promoted by your superiors, clearly demonstrate your gratitude but cleverly reject this offer. If you are unsatisfied with your position and intend to leave, stay there impermanently to create a mysterious hallucination for others. Changing your audible speech and visible actions as a rotating sphere in order to confuse others and mislead them about your intention. In this scenario, "retreat" is the core principle.

$$Chapter\ 4.$$

Di Xi

(Blocking the Hole)

All beings are subject to unique evolutionary doctrines, and all things are determined by the laws of union and division. Some people, who are in the vicinity of our physical spaces, fail to trigger our attention. Others who are farther away in great distance but can easily establish connection and mutual understanding with us. The reason that some are ignored by us is because we do not attentively examine their words and languages. Additionally, the reason that others can be understood is because we associate with each other on a frequent basis so that we are conscious of our characters.

"Xi" means small hole, which grows in humble magnitude, but can expands into earth-cracking fissure. When the small hole first emerges, it is crucial to barricade it, which is the definition of "Di". There are numerous usages of such techniques, you can diminish it, repel it, or extinguish it. The ultimate goal is to achieve victory. As described above, this is the law of "Di Xi".

When encountering perilous incidents, only the Great Man is able to discern and understand them, and capitalizes their benefits exclusively. He can analyze affairs and objects by their changes, adept at employing strategies, and fathom details just from surface. All incidents begin as tiny and insignificant as small feathers that grow under birds' wings, but can enlarge to something as massive and titanic as Mount. Himalayas' foundation. After the benevolent policies of the Great Man have been administrated, the malevolent schemes of the cunning scoundrels can be countered by the law of "Di Xi". Therefore, blocking small holes and extinguishing them---is both an art and a science.

When the world is shattering and the sky is falling, sinister manifestations such as incompetent leaders and immoral barons loom from the shadows. Thus cunning scoundrels will take advantage of such opportunity to pour poisons in the ears of King, which result in distrusted and abused people of talent and virtue. The Great Man flees to hide from chaos, while the avaricious and fraudulent mongrels smash the world to smithereens. The bond of trust between the lord and the minister cracks, causing universal constitutions to splinter to dust. Civilians bombard and murder each other, father and son terminate their relationship, and even siblings resent and slaughter their own kin. Such are the harbinger of a widening "Xi". When the Great Man sense its emergence, he will utilize of law of "Di Xi" to prevent any more damages and halt the fissure. For instance, if the world can still be restored to its former glory, the Great Man will block the small hole, attempt

   WISDOM OF THE GHOST VALLEY

to heal its wound in order to ensure its survivability. On the other hand, if the world has fallen to oblivion, then he will break the fissure, completely destroy it in order to rebuild a new one that he dominates. In the same manner, the law of "Di Xi" can also be applied to repair the world, conquer the world, revive the world or replace the world. According to legends, the ancient world of China was repaired to a new height of advancement in the age of the Five Emperors. Correspondingly, the original world of China was conquered and established in the age of the Three Sovereigns. Warring and belligerent lords who are constantly clashing against each other are beyond numbers. In this era, those who gain mastery over the law of "Di" "Xi" are bound to victory.

Ever since the heaven and earth possess aspects such as union, division, beginning and end, small holes and fissures unavoidably coexist with all things and all beings, which is of vital importance to be precisely examined and observed. To accomplish that, one must utilize the law of "Bai He". And that one...is the irreplaceable Great Man. He is the peculiar messenger of the heaven and earth. If the world is functioning normally without any holes to remedy, then he will conceal himself in the darkest shadow to wait for the perfect opportunity. However, if the world has demonstrated signs of fracture and instability, then he will prepare and strategize in order to fully repair the world to its peak. Therefore, he can cooperate with his superiors while monitoring his subordinates with unparalleled confidence, which derives from the authority of the law of "Di Xi" that he strictly adheres to. That man, arms with such unmatched wisdom, is the very embodiment of the "Celestial Protector of the Heaven and Earth".

Chapter 5.

———❦———

Fei Qian

(The Flying Pincer)

The purpose of assessing intelligence and evaluating capabilities is to attract competent professionals and employ them, which then inducing them to fully commit themselves to your cause. First and foremost, establishing decree and managing business are depend on your mental acuity to understand their similarities and differences in order to penetrate fact and gossip. Then, you shall unravel their superficial lies and innermost truths to better comprehend their potential and deficiencies. Additionally, you shall determine the vital strategy of the country's survivability and decide the relationship between superiors and subordinates. Moreover, you shall initiate the judgment of each person's strengths and weaknesses. After the evaluation is complete, the employment process can commence. It has several criteria: acceptance; promotion; and premium. When negotiating with your opponents, it is critical to utilize the words of "Qian" (which means pincers) such as temptation and provocation, to capture their hearts in a blink of an eye. The art of "Fei Qian" is a type of Persuasion Technique, featuring rapid changes in verbal languages that match or differ the opponents'. As for those who cannot be subdued by it, intimidate or bribe them first, and then repeatedly test them-their desires, characters, philosophies, frustrations and relationships. Or reverse the order-test them first and then annihilate them. For some, such repeated assessments can yield distraction, demoralization and destruction of the opponents. For others, it is precisely the damage done to the opponents that produce these assessments. When attempting to employ someone, enticing them with abundant money, luxurious commodities, sumptuous treasures, priceless jewelries, luminous gems, delicate silks, or extravagant goods. Likewise, measuring their abilities first, which then can be used to create a desirable circumstance that capture them permanently. Furthermore, you shall scrutinize and discover their weaknesses in order to dominate them with pincer-like accuracy. As described above, these methods can be utilized with the accompaniment of the law of "Di Xi".

In order to preach the art of "Fei Qian" to the whole world, you must make conscientious judgment about people-their intelligence and competence. You shall also fathom the prosperity and decline of time, understand geographical characteristics and its implications on trade and politics, recognize mountain ridges and terrain altitude's peculiarity, and appreciate the total wealth of the people. In addition, the intriguing and complicated relationship between the lords themselves, must be thoroughly studied:

                    WISDOM OF THE GHOST VALLEY

who are intimate, who are distant, who are friendly, who are hostile, and what are their deepest concerns and cravings. Again, you should perceive the opponents' intentions and understand their preferences to fluently persuade them on what they care the most. Utilizing the words of "Fei", the sheer speed, to lure out their desires, and then utilize the words of "Qian", the indominable pincer, to control them and ultimately get what you want.

To use such techniques on others, you must first observe their intelligence and capabilities, measure their authority and power, anticipate their energy and force, and then precisely capture their vulnerability to either welcome or comply them without causing them realize that it is a feigned agreement and trust. After that, utilize the law of "Qian" to reach mutual compromise and harmonious relationship with that intention to achieve the ideal results. Such is the profound application of the art of "Fei Qian".

To use such techniques on human relationships, manipulate others with vain but extravagant words of compliment in order to reveal their true intention and intelligence. Then immediately utilize this perfect opportunity to meticulously scrutinize the real meaning behind their words, and relentlessly assault their weak spots with the sheer force of pincers in order to verbally, emotionally and spiritually dominate them, forcing them to you will. There is absolutely no limit regard of the numerous practices of the art of "Fei Qian". For instance, you can forge and break alliances, educate and brainwash civilians, guide and mislead subordinates, and even entice and ruin superiors. Although potent and resourceful, the art of "Fei Qian" should be applied with caution and remember never breach its propriety or boundary.

Chapter 6.

(A or B)

REGARDLESS OF FORGING alliance or breaking accord, appropriate strategies are always needed. They change and rotate like iron rings, connecting and unbreakable while adjusting and formless. On the other hand, situations and opponents change by seconds, and even the largest of them often depend on the tiniest factors. Decisions, then, must be made based on facts. Therefore, the Great Man who resides amongst the heaven and earth, erects himself and dominates the world in order to educate the public, expand his influence and augment his reputation. Meanwhile, he will analyze the relationship of changes between beings, and perceive both the value and significance of time to execute his ambitions without any delay. Lastly, he shall thoroughly understand the strengths, weaknesses, cultures and characteristics of the target country to prophesize potential changes and adjust his plan according to his best interest.

The world has no eternal virtue, and things has no defined log-ics. The Great Man, therefore, does everything possible and hears anything audible. And the main principle will always be achieving guaranteed victory while matching the core strategy. However, it is no surprise that the opponents' benefits will always be your costs. When there is friendship, there is betrayal. Such is the nature of all strategies: duality-winning and losing coexist for both sides. Therefore, pleasing one side will displease the other, and vise versa. This contradicting nature is precisely the founda-tion of the law of "Wu He". To utilize it to operate the whole world, you must assess based on international perspective and relationships first and then take actions. Similarly, using it to gov-ern a specific country requires that you must know the accurate information about the target country before making decisions; using it to manage family demands that you must comprehend its desires and struggles to solve its problems; and using it to master yourself obliges that you must understand you ambition, mind-set and circumstances to truly unleash "Wu He's" full potential. Consequently, its functions and applications remain the same no matter the magnitude of the incidents or the circumstance you are facing. Therefore, it is crucial to make intelligent judgment and long-term decisions before evaluating which strategies con-tributes to the best interest, and then utilize the law of "Fei Qian" to materialize the desired results.

The ancient masters who exceled in the art of both treachery and allegiance, could effortlessly balance the world, accept lords of all kind, achieve the pinnacle of "Wu He", and then change their

　　　　WISDOM OF THE GHOST VALLEY

mentalities, loyalty, and strategies in order to create a new era of truth and prosperity. Therefore, Yi Yin served Emperor Tang of Shang Dynasty for five times and also served King Jie of Xia Dynasty for five times before he made the final decision to pledge his loyalty to Tang in order to defeat Jie, thus marking the beginning of Shang Dynasty. Likewise, Jiang Ziya once served both the Duke of Zhou and Di Xin of Shang thrice. After witnessing his corrupted and ruthless nature and the decline of Shang Dynasty, Jiang Ziya decided to swear his loyalty to the Duke of Zhou. These two knew their destinies to the very core so that they could surrender themselves to the wise leaders without any doubts. Correspondingly, those who do not possess virtue and wisdom that are parallel to the Great Mans, cannot govern the whole world; those who do not exhaust themselves to thinking and reflecting, cannot comprehend the true nature of things; those who do not observe details with laser-beam focus, cannot achieve glory or fame; those who lack intelligence or competence cannot strategize military decisions; and those who are too simple and naïve that fail to perceive truths behind lies, cannot know people well. As a result, the art of "Wu He" can only be applied after measuring your own intelligence and capabilities, and comparing them with others' strengths, weaknesses, visions and philosophies in order to discern what you are lacking. Only then can you advance, retreat, forge or break alliances as smooth as water.

Chapter 7.

Chuai

(Assess)

The ancient masters, who were adept in world domination and management, always assessed the international situations first, and then evaluated the lords and their schemes. Unable to carefully measure the world, on the other hand, will result in failure to understand the lords: their strengths, weaknesses, truth, and deceit. Similarly, unable to fathom true intel of things will result in inability to comprehend the situations: its changes, developments, movement and stillness. How can you exactly measure situations? The answer is evaluating advantages and disadvantages, and strategizing edges and losses. In addition, you should calculate wealth, predict citizens' affluence and penury, and estimate the difference between them. You shall also distinguish the geographical characteristics: its hazard, plateau, and its relevant importance and peril. Furthermore, you shall contemplate your strategies: their advantages and disadvantages; you shall perceive the relationship between superiors and subordinates: who are in alliance with whom, who are virtuous and who are despicable; you shall discern the patrons: who are intelligent and who are foolish; you shall observe the weather and its prophecies: which implies fortune and which implies misfortune; you shall comprehend the lords and their intentions: who can be trusted and who cannot be trusted; you shall understand the civilians and their hearts: why they form communities, why they depart, what makes such changes, how do they contribute to the safety or danger on a greater scale, what do they desire, and what do they abhor, which, without doubts, can be the direct clues to predict their insurrections. Only after you have mastered the above acumens can you then call yourself a true strategist. The definition of "Chuai" is understanding truths and facts. For instance, you should greatly inflate your opponents' desires when they are at the peak of their bliss. Since their desires dominate them, which then prevent any possibilities of escape or camouflage. Besides, you should greatly escalate their fears when they are at the depths of their terror. Since their fears dominate them, which then also inhibit any possibilities of escape or camouflage. Such emotions will sure lose to changes of the circumstances. For those whose emotions are moved but do not demonstrate any signs of changes on their languages or expressions, it is best to neglect them and do not speak to them for now but approach their closest friends and families instead, understanding why they remain in this way and what their emotional reliance are. Additionally, for people whose emotions undergo changes internally, it is unavoidable that they manifest them on their appearances and behaviors. Therefore, it is crucial to comprehend the "subsurface" of their iceberg from their "surface", which correspond to hidden truths and superficial manifestations. Such is the art of "Chuai"-in-depths examination and understanding.

Therefore, those who strategize the whole country must delicately measure their own authorities and powers. When persuading foreign kings, you should thoroughly assess their intel and facts, which are the keys to understand their schemes, thoughts, emotions and desires. Only then can you truly comprehend the art of "Chuai" and apply it to respective targets splendidly. Hence you can respect them, belittle them, regard them, ignore them, bribe them, damage them, glorify them or ruin them-through the same principle. Accordingly, even though you might possess the benevolent character of ancient kings and supreme intelligence of a Great Man, you will still unable to discern the secretive intel without utilizing the method of "Chuai". This is the core principle of all strategies and the main law of the Persuasion Techniques. Oftentimes incidents happen to people but they fail to predict beforehand because it is most difficult to forecast such occurrences in advance. Therefore, mastering the art of "Chuai" is the most challenging task due to the perfect timing to speak and persuade, which is decided by careful planning. In comparison, when insect larva first crawl above their holes, all of their movements are the results of survival instinct: benefit first, and harm last. They are the indication of changes of details that foretell the development of propensity. All things and beings are small and insignificant when they are born or created. These mechanisms of "Chuai" should be embellished with lavish words and incorporated in complete articles, which will be discussed in later chapters.

Chapter 8.

(Evaluate)

"Mo" is the technical application of "Chuai". In this scenario, internal emotional transformation and external behavioral manifestation are the main signs of change. You should utilize the law of "Mo" with rigorous adherence to secrecy. When first using this technique, you shall mildly incorporate the law of "Mo" to your mindset and languages to understand the opponents' desires, and then continue to spy and observe their reactions till their external factors match their internal ones. Meanwhile, they will always perform some actions that reveal their hidden emotions, which then can be deciphered with "Mo". After this procedure is completed, you may need to intentionally ignore and leave them in order to conceal your movements, vanish your traces, camouflage your appearances, and dodge their intelligence. Such masterful disguise is the reason why others have no clue about you, which assuredly contribute to your success while vanquishing your restlessness. The main principle is to discern the opponents to trigger their inner selves. If successful, then there is nothing that cannot be accomplished.

The ancient masters who were fluent in the art of "Mo", corresponded to the movement of launching the hook to catch fish in the bottom of abyss. As long as he brought delicious baits and casted it into the water, he was guaranteed to get a big one. Therefore, the main objective is progressively achieved without letting anyone know; the military purpose is deliberately attained without frightening anyone. The Great Man consciously hatches his plots in the shadows, so it is paralleled as omnipotence. But then he accomplishes his goals and every knows in the light, so it is correlated as transparency. As a result, those who progressively achieved the main objective clandestinely accumulate their virtue and character, and the civilians who enjoy peace and prosperity fail to understand the reasons behind all these benefits. This is the perfect demonstration of how they become so virtuous and honorable. If the civilians appreciate and cherish in this moment without a single clue of the current occurrence, then the whole world praises such administrations of "shadow and light" as godlike and omniscient. In the same way, the military commanders who deliberately attain victory, often battle their opponents without transpiring serious confrontations or wasting needless resources. Therefore, the civilians often do not understand why the opponents surrender themselves or fear to engage in combat, which is why the whole world praises such tactics of "shadow and light" as godlike and omnipotent.

When employing the techniques of "Mo", you can negotiate with your opponents about peace, accuse them in the name of justice, please them with entertainment, provoke their rage and fury, threaten them with reputation, force them with certain actions, move them with honesty, persuade them with trust, bribe them with goods and money, and weaken their doubts with humility. Peace derives from tranquility; justice derives from straightforwardness; entertainment derives from pleasure; rage derives from passion; reputation derives from influence; action derives from execution; honesty derives from cleanness; trust derives from transparency; bribe derives from greed and humility derives from flattery. Therefore, the art of "Chuai" and "Mo", which was exclusively manipulated by the Great Man, is now accessible to all people. However, the reason that those who still fail to yield significant result is because they do not apply it properly. As a result, there are no strategies more challenging than meticulous planning, there is no persuasion more difficult than all acceptances, and there are no objectives more difficult than guaranteed fulfillment. Only those who have mastered all of the three crafts described above can be defined as intelligent and competent.

Therefore, you must strategize your plan with scrupulous consideration, you must choose the appropriate targets of similar interest when lobbying, which is why you would like to form an unbreakable and amiable connection with them. If you truly want to accomplish your objective, then you must integrate the art of "Chuai" and "Mo" to your operation. Accordingly, the only condition required for accomplishment is when the principle, execution and time match perfectly. So if you want your targets to listen to your appeal, you must make you argument appropriate to their emotions and desires, which if applied accurately, almost always result an assured triumph. Therefore, all things belong to their own categories, which is similar to you carry woods to extinguish fire and the dry bulks incinerate first. When you pour water on the ground, the hollowed pit drenches first. Such are examples of phenomenon that harmonize with the objects' characteristics, and at that situation, it is unquestionably to occur. In accordance with this principle, people's inner and emotional transformations will materialize to their external and apparent expressions. Therefore, you shall evaluate and assess the traits of things to employ the art of "Mo", and understand which parts are not congruent with their exhibiting behaviors. Also, you shall utilize the art of "Mo" based on your opponents' desires and intentions, thus guaranteeing your proposals to be approved. In conclusion, such brilliant and sophisticated art can only be comprehended by the Great Man. As for those who are extremely ambitious in politics and distinguished in strategies, they shall not waste any opportunities, and remain calm and collected after achieving greatness. And then in time, they will ultimately accomplish their goals-changing the world.

Chapter 9.

Quan

(GAUGE)

THE PURPOSE OF persuasion is to influence others, which is then meant to benefit you. Those decorative and beautifying words are only vain lies, but can be either beneficial or detrimental according to your current circumstance. When responding to others, you must be eloquent and fluent in your diplomatic speech that is superficial by nature. On the other hand, those words of truth and faith must be thoughtfully differentiated to test which one is genuine and can be trusted. Those words of condemnation and criticism are meant to challenge and inflame others, which then can be used to lure out their hidden secrets. People who speak words of flattery and adulation want to appear to be loyal; people who speak words of utopian abstruseness want to appear to be intellectual; people who speak words of brutal honesty appear to be bold due to their decisiveness; people who speak words of somber melancholy and are in an authoritative position want to appear to be trustworthy; people who speak words of reserved calmness hide their own flaws and blame others to appear to be victorious. Those who intend to realize their incentives and blandish others with fancy words are flatterers. Those who frequently quote abstract and scholastic terms from classic tomes are pretenders. Those who purposely conspire schemes and advise flawed strategies for their superiors are usurpers. Those who abandon certain benefits without a single thought of doubt are decision makers. Those who are originally erroneous but instead blame others for their own faults are deniers.

Therefore, mouth is the origin of our verbal languages. It can be used to announce or block emotions and information. Ears and eyes are the supports of mind so that they can discern treachery and evil. Accordingly, as long as mind, eyes and ears collaborate with each other, you will step in the road to your success. As a result, you shall not be disoriented when hearing annoying and bothersome words; you shall not be befuddled when listening to eloquent and pervasive words; you shall not be afraid of changes in either languages or structures because you can capture the vital points and then comprehend the whole rationale. So for those who are blind or short-sighted, it is unnecessary to show them different colors of life. For those who are deaf or unintelligent listeners, it is unnecessary discuss music of life with them. Therefore, you do not need to approach these people because they are unambitious and unworthy to be enlightened; you do not need to persuade them because they are foolish and unwilling to welcome new ideas. There are things in the world that are just

WISDOM OF THE GHOST VALLEY

incommunicable or unintelligible, which is why they can never accomplish greatness. There is an old saying: the mouth is used to eat, but not to speak. Because words can easily offend others, and the ancient analogy "words of crowd melt gold" implies the same meaning: languages twist facts and obscure truths.

Speaking out loud and wishing others to listen is human nature. The same applies to executing objectives and wishing guaranteed success. Therefore, an intelligent person does not utilize his weaknesses, but instead uses a fool's strengths. He does not employ his deficiency, but rather employs a fool's expertise. This is the reason why he never encounters a difficult situation that he cannot solve. When speaking of others' strengths, you shall fully augment theirs, and when speaking of others' weaknesses, you shall speedily avoid theirs. As a result, the beetle uses its strong and hard carapace to defend itself. And the scorpion uses its poisonous and deadly sting to paralyze its prey. From this perspective, even the wild beasts know how to utilize their advantages, so the speaker must understand the application of the persuasion techniques.

Therefore, there are five categories of the persuasion technique: words of sickness, words of sorrow, words of apprehension, words of rage, and words of gratification. Words of sickness are languages that are tainted by impotent energies and spiritual deterioration. Words of sorrow are languages that are clouded by heartbroken melancholy that unable to find salvation. Words of apprehension are languages that are sealed by mental obstruction thus cannot vent it out loud. Words of rage are languages that are bloodied by irrational judgment which are out of the control of the speaker himself. And lastly, words of gratification are languages that are seduced by nonchalant attitude that are anything but significant or intelligent. Those above fives, can only be applied after you have truly mastered their essentials and can only be executed when the situation is beneficial. Therefore, when speaking with the wise, you should rely on wisdom; when speaking with the fool, you should rely on squabble; when speaking with the lobbyist, you should rely on principles; when speaking with the sophisticated, you should rely on impression; when speaking with the rich, you should rely on elegance; when speaking with the poor, you should rely on benefits; when speaking with the despicable, you should rely on humility; when speaking with the brave, you should rely on assertiveness; when speaking with the flawed, you should rely on resourcefulness. Such are the techniques of fundamental human communications, which, on the contrary, are always used adversely by many. Consequently, when speaking to intelligent people, you shall first make them clearly understand these principles first. And when speaking to foolish people, even though you attempt to educate them with these principles, it is far too difficult to accomplish that. So there are many approaches of the Persuasion Techniques, as there are many forms of the change of things. After you have learned this, you can speak for the whole day without deviating from the main principle or jeopardizing the objective. On the other hand, even if you remain silent for the whole day, you can still keep your character and let your doctrine prevail. As a result, the wise are most valuable because they are calm and collected. They listen to differentiate the truths and lies, they think to understand the rights and wrongs, and they speak to demonstrate the element of surprise.

Chapter 10.

Mou

(STRATEGIZE)

ALL STRATEGIES ARE based on one principle-understanding the causes. So that you can grasp true intel from the surface. After this, you shall establish Three Doctrines: superiority-invisible strategies that accomplish objectives without letting anyone know, mediocrity-strategies that accomplish objectives with certain costs and loses, and inferiority-involuntary but mandatory plans that fix problems at a great cost on yourself. Combine these three and you will be able to surprise your opponents at will. Such ambushes can penetrate the deepest veil, leave nothing to hide. This tactic has been proven to be victorious from the ancient times. Therefore, people of ancient Zheng often brought wagons that had installed compasses with them when they mined gems in the mountains so that they would never lose their directions. On the same manner, evaluating talents, measuring capabilities, and fathoming information should mirror the principle of utilizing compass. For that reason, those who share similar interests and befriend with each other are both successful in multiple areas; those who share similar interests but distant from each other are damaged in some areas; those who abhor each other but remain close in contact are threatened by a common foe; and those who abhor each other while keeping the distance are only threatened on one side. As a result, when there is benefit, there is collaboration; and when there is damage, there is segregation. Such is the law that not only has been proven countless times, but also serves as a means to differentiate friends and foes, and categorize things and beings. Therefore, walls collapse because of cracks, and trees fall because of breaking. It is certain to happen. Consequently, changes breed objectives, objectives breed strategies, strategies breed plans, plans breed discussions, discussions breed persuasions, persuasions breed advances, advances breed retreats, retreats breed principles, which is used to control the situation. In conclusion, all things adhere to one principle that no matter how many repetitions or variations, it will always remain unchanged.

A man of virtue always belittles to the temptation of coins, so you cannot bribe them with money but can convince them to donate their wealth. A man of valor always belittles to the challenge of adversity, so you cannot frighten them with anxiety but can compel them to fortify a hazardous position. A man of wisdom excels in courtesy and comprehends all principles, so you cannot feign honesty to them but can speak reasons with them in order to drive them to accomplish greatness. This is the definition of "three talents": virtue, valor, and wisdom. Therefore, a fool can

 WISDOM OF THE GHOST VALLEY

easily be manipulated, a coward can easily be frightened, and a beggar can easily be bribed. So you shall decide which strategy to employ based on different circumstances. As a result, the strong is accumulated by the weak, and the abundant is accumulated by the scarce. Such is the expression of the art of "Mou".

Therefore, when facing those who are friendly on the surface but aloof in the heart, you shall speak the language of inner feelings. When facing those who friendly in the heart but distant on the surface, you shall speak the language of outer appearance. So you should change your vocabularies based on your opponents' doubts; you should respond based on your opponents' expressions and behaviors; you should conclude your main arguments from the words of your opponents; you should gratify your opponents based on the change of the circumstance; you should you dominate your opponents based on what they hate; and you should repel things that they concern. After you finished evaluating them, threaten them with harms, elevate and persuade them, slightly back up your claims with proof, respond them after they have matched your assumptions, block their words after advocating them (so that you can lure them into your territory), and bewitch them after harassing them. These are the implications of "Mou". As for its actual application, secrecy is better than publicity, and party is even better secrecy-because such parties are united without rifts. Unpredictable and intelligent strategies are better than the ordinary ones because they flood your opponents with unstoppable force. As a result, when persuading Kings, you shall discuss such strategies with them first, and when persuading the officials, you shall forge a secretive relationship with them first.

Even though you are of the same side with one group but choose to speak to the benefit of the other, you will be repelled and isolated. If you are an outside who knows too much about insider's secrets, you will put yourself in a very dangerous situation. Do not attempt to force others to accept what they dislike. Do not educate others about what they do not understand. If they have a certain type of passion or hobby, you shall imitate to match theirs. If they have a certain type of disgust or hatred, you shall avoid discussing such topics. So you shall use a Persuasion Technique in the shadow and reap the desired results in the light. Therefore, if you want to completely eliminate someone, you should first spoil them rotten and let them do anything they please-with the intention to eradicate them once they reveal their fatal flaws. Those who never expose their emotions outside, whether it is joy or rage, are calm and reserved individuals, whom you can trust with great responsibility. For those who you know by heart, you can trust and use them; for those who you do not know by heart, you cannot trust or use them from a strategic perspective. As a result, it is imperative to control other people, and it is lethal to be controlled by them. Those who control other people are omnipotent shepherds, and those who are controlled by other people are impotent sheep. Consequently, the Great Men employ the art of strategies in the shadows, while the fools squawk their amateur schemes in the light. The wise accomplish their goals with ease, whereas the fools struggle to get started. From this point of view, the dead cannot be revived, and the chaos cannot be pacified. Therefore, "Wu Wei" and "Wisdom" are of utmost importance. Intelligence should be used on where no one can understand, and competence should be used on where no one can see. After displaying intelligence and competence, if they are proven to be beneficial, you shall choose the right time to do the right thing-this is for your own gains. If, on the other hand, they are not beneficial, you shall again choose the right time to do the right thing-this is for others' gains. Therefore, the ancient ways of Kings value secrecy more than anything else. As the saying goes: "the heaven and earth evolve on height and depth, and the way of the Great Man augment on secrecy and concealment. Not purely based on loyalty, integrity, benevolence, or justice. It is just a means to maintain the public image of appropriateness. If other people can truly comprehend the truth of this principle, you can speak with them. If both of you acknowledge and appreciate each other, then you can forge both current and long-term relationships with them.

Chapter 11.
Jue
(Decision-Making)

When making decisions, it is crucial that you rely on contemplation. Accept fortune and happiness, and reject danger and apprehension. If the harms exceed temptation, then you will finally vanquish all doubts. All offers have some kinds of benefits, if they are eliminated, however, then according to your resourcefulness and justification, you shall never accept them. If a person who seems to adhere to the principle of benevolence, but secretly does actions of evil, then you shall not accept him-his personality, languages, or offers. Although this may cause you to separate from each other, if you tolerate him to damage your benefits or wreak havoc on both you and your relationships, then that would truly be a mistake in decision making. The reasons that the Great Man is able to accomplish greatness are: inspire and encourage people (the way of "yang" virtue), execute and assassinate people (the way of "yin" cruelty), preach the honor of trust and integrity, protect the needed and vulnerable people with love, and purify people with honesty and chastity. The way of "yang" emphasizes on the aspect of consistency and persistence of a single perspective of an object, whereas the way of "yin" emphasizes on the aspect of mastery and benefits of the dual perspectives of an object. You should craftly utilize these principles in both ordinary and crucial situations with caution. Therefore, you shall measure and compare old incidents in the past in order to examine and prove the new incidents in the future. And then you should assess your opponents based on their mundane languages and behaviors. If it is beneficial to the results, then you can make the decision. As for the affairs of Kings and aristocrats, if your actions are risky but can contribute to your reputation, then you can make the decision; if your actions are effortless to complete and the results are easy to achieve, then you can make the decision; if your actions are laborious and strenuous but at the same time necessary and decisive, then you can make the decision; if your actions can eliminate disasters, then you can make the decision; if your actions can realize fortune and happiness, then you can make the decision. Therefore, assessing situations and intelligence, and solving difficulties and anxieties are the crucial points of smoothly accomplishing all things. Governing people based on right and wrong and making decisions that ultimately impact victory or defeat-is truly a difficult task. As a result, the ancient Kings used yarrow flowers and turtle shells to make decision by themselves.

Chapter 12.

(WAYS OF SELF-MASTERY)

IF A PERSON of status can achieve peace, calmness, righteousness, and tranquility, then his character and intellect will naturally reach a level of brilliance. If you are altruistic but struggle to find inner peace, then you should humble your heart and calm your spirit to wait for the collapse and downfall of certain people or country. This is the definition of strategically remaining in your position.

Eyes shall be bright, ears shall be sharp, and mind shall be acute. There is nothing invisible if you project the whole world's view into your own eyes; there is nothing inaudible if you project the whole world's hearing into your own ears; and there is nothing unintelligible if you project the whole world's thought into your own mind. Therefore, if all people in the world concentrate their eyes, ears, and minds and rush forward together like car wheels, then their clarity and intelligence cannot be stopped. This is the definition of crystal-transparent clarity.

The technique of listening: don't assert your own opinions so much that you reject others. Accepting advices from others creates a barrier of protection, while denying advices from others creates a block of obstruction. Staring mountains upward and you can see the summit. Measuring bottom of the lake and you can assess it scale. However, a god's mentality is both righteous and perceptive, therefore it is impossible to measure. This is the definition of Emperor's acceptance.

When rewarding others, it is essential to keep your promise. When punishing others, it is essential to make decisions based on fairness and justice. As mentioned above, it is imperative to let people witness and listen such occasions of promotion to verify the trustworthiness of your words. As for those who do not witness by their owns eyes or listen by their own ears, your promise of rewards has an indirect and subconscious influence on them. If your honesty and integrity can preach the whole world and everyone understands, then even the gods themselves will protect you, and why are you afraid of treacherous scoundrels who would invade your crown? This is the definition of trustworthy rewards and punishments.

Time, place and human. Four directions: left, right, front, and back. Where exactly is Mars? You should be familiar of all of them. This is the definition of know-it-all.

   WISDOM OF THE GHOST VALLEY

The mind is the ruler of your body, and the King is the ruler of all officials. People whose deeds are beneficial should be rewarded, whereas people whose deeds are detrimental should be punished. The king employs talents based on their achievements. And he offers handsome rewards according to real progresses and circumstances so that no civilians will ever complain and the treasury is secure. The Great Man, therefore, uses these people in order to better control them. By adhering to these solid principles, the kingdom can last long. This is the definition of adherence of principles.

As the rule of all people, you must approach and understand the outside world and its ever-changing aspects. If you are deficient in human relationships, then it is very likely that your subordinates wreak chaos. It is unnatural for the world to remain in total silence. If you neither communicate nor contact with the internal (your personal) and external (the outside) worlds, then how can you understand the changes that are undergoing in the current era? Inappropriate uses of openness and closedness can result in failure of understanding of the principles of all things. This is the definition of common awareness.

Far-seeing, far-hearing, and timber-clarity. Across thousand miles, among the impenetrable veils and imperceptible tones, lies the all-knowing eyes of the wise. The evils of all worlds can never escape him even in the shadows. This is the definition of discerning the evil.

Act according to the benefits of your reputation, and finish when it is in fact safe and sound. Reputation and facts born out of each other, but complement perfectly with logic and emotions. Therefore, the saying goes: reputation is born from fact, fact is born from truth, truth is born from the virtue of the combination of reputation and fact, virtue is born from peace, and peace is born from appropriateness and fairness. This is the definition of harmony between reputation and fact.

Chapter 13.

Zhuan Wan

(Twisting the Sphere)

This chapter is lost to ages.

Chapter 14.

Que Kuan

(Calming Chaos)

This chapter is lost to ages.

CONTACT INFORMATION

Translator's Name: Jack Sun

Email: contactjacksun@gmail.com

Facebook: Jack Sun

LinkedIn: Jack Sun